The
BLACK
BOOK
OF
BLACK

The Battle of History
can only be fought with TRUTH

poetry   aj houston

Not Just Alphabets Publishing

Las Vegas, Nevada

All Not Just Alphabets Publishing titles, AJ Houston, wordart, imprints and lines distributed are available at special quantity discounts for bulk purchases for sales promotion, fund raising, premiums, educational, institutional and library use.

Copyright © 2015 by AJ Houston. All rights reserved.

No part of this work may be reproduced or transmitted in any form or by any means, electronic or mechanical, including photocopying and recording, or by any information storage retrieval system without the prior written permission of A.J. Houston or Not Just Alphabets. Email notjustalphabets@gmail.com address to Permissions.

Printed in the U. S. A.

Library of Congress Catalog Card Number: 9963124-3

ISBN: 978-0-9963129- 4- 3

Dedication:

To my seeds and anyone searching to understand why writers with melanin will refer to matters of conscience, unity, community, slavery, pain and a struggle no one else believes is or was ever there... why each grouping of words will read as if they were written more than three hundred years ago, bearing new names and references. History has a long term effect if the resolve is never resolved or addressed. Dear History... we are on our way, don't give up.

Introduction

I sat proud and honored as I passed her the pages of what I considered to be one of my best pieces to date. Waiting in silence for her opinion, it took a lot less time than I believed was possible to read to completion. In anticipation, I watched her lips as she opened her mouth to offer her conclusion... she turned, smiled brightly, saying...
"oh, its alright; but this is just another slave poem."

I think it was about five years ago, I started writing notes to begin "The Book of Niggaz". The title couldn't have changed if I wanted to change it. Every person of African descent wore the title after their arrival here. For the book to have meaning it would have to be in the form of truth. I imagined it being this great work, a record documenting history in verse from boarding the first ship to present day. The project and process came to a halt in 2013 after reading a new miniseries would be airing on local television called "The Book of Negroes". I find it intriguing how writers not in association with each other will come up with similar titles or ideas. It seems concepts and ideas visit various people to see who has the best follow through. Everything you write will have a brother or sister in thought from a region you have never visited, or presented by a person you never had the pleasure of meeting. Don't take it personal if you happen to hear someone read a poem, publish a book, write a blog or article bearing the same title you thought was uniquely yours. Some thoughts demand to be written and will not wait on you to get it done.

I have witnessed this occurrence more than twice, while working on a project in secret someone comes out with its identical twin. Some may call it coincidence but I consider it a cosmic event. Your follow through must be refined to meet the demands of life. There are stories needing to be told, it will not matter the lips from which they fall. Think of Fate as a door to door salesman visiting writers, non-writers, singers, musicians and rappers laying out in clear view the best ideas offering no contract but giving you an option to buy. Even after purchasing you will not own the rights until you complete the task. Reality is a hard pill to swallow especially when you would rather choose not to take the medicine. It is easier to label yourself a writer than to write. The amount of due diligence required to walk a plan from beginning to completion will often be disenchanting at the least.

"The Black Book of Black", is somewhat a reversion in an offbeat kind of way to "The Book of Niggaz". The format of this book is completely different from the original idea, enclosed you will see excerpts mentally recalled from the unwritten first book. Believe me, I really did try and find a more palatable title, but there wasn't one available to convey the weight of the content needed to insure believability. Hopefully I won't be held completely accountable for the way the words leaped from my pen. The rule of writing is: in order to get more to write about you must follow the demands of the words given and entrusted in your care. These words and verses all of them were definitely given to me. Leaving me to question whether to quit writing all together, or write no matter what I thought of the content inserted in my pen.

I find joy every day in the gifts received by my fingers, I will never consider myself the origin of any of the thoughts presented and forever thankful to write them is my mantra. Poetry is a gift of sorts, a blessing to hands, the praise dancing of fingers. I consider myself blessed and honored completely to write whatever appears in front of me. Thank you for joining me in this quest for knowledge, this path of truly attempting to get better at the art of designing thoughts.

Welcome to "The Black Book of Black"

Table of Contents

In The Beginning 9

History From A Child's Perspective 16

Nightmares' 20

Conversations With The Ancestors 24

Harriett 30

Excerpt From The Unwritten Book "The Book of Niggaz"
Charter 3 (Home) verses 1: – 8: 34

Disconnect 36

This Is What Happens When You Bootleg Freedom 38

Some Better 44

Excerpt From The Unwritten Book "The Book of Niggaz"
Charter 12 (The Journey) verses 7: – 12: 47

When My Ancestors Come 48

Action 53

How Can You Listen 56

Excerpt From The Unwritten Book "The Book of Niggaz"
Charter 18 (of Water and Rain) verses 27: – 33: 60

Where Is The God In You (2) 62

Sentry's of Sand 66

Talking Drums 71

Roar 75

Excerpt From The Unwritten Book "The Book of Niggaz"
Charter 26 (No More Sun) verses 81: – 88: 78

Matters of Fact 80

Dark and Darkness 85

Hell or What 90

Excerpt From The Unwritten Book "The Book of Niggaz"
Charter 48 (Next) verses 22: – 28: 95

Questions and Answers 97

Heaven and Home 104

The Slave Trees 109

Excerpt From The Unwritten Book "The Book of Niggaz"
Charter 62 (Afterlife) verses 136: – 150: 113

Dirt 119

This Is The Last Time I fix Broken (2) 122

Cotton 125

Just Wanted A passing Grade 129

Complicated 134

History In 76 Lines (From beginning To New Beginning) 140

Takeaways and Notes or Negro Spirituals 143

Biography 145

Acknowledgements 146

Product Information 147

Contact Information 148

The Black Book of Black

Texas had the largest production of cotton in the U.S. between 2010 and 2012, it produced almost 5.5 million bales. A bale of cotton weighs approximately 485 to 500 pounds.

A Cotton Ball... average weight 0.5 grams

Our new mantra should be:
"Never Again" or history will circle back and remind us not to forget.

In The Beginning

I think it goes back

to the beginning

before word split darkness

to form night and day

we were there and are still here

trying to find our way to the light

I would try and go back

to the beginning

or at least as far as my mind

will enable me to remember

I don't recall thinking about

being able to walk or talk

never paid attention

to air or breathing

no one told me I had to

we have a long list of givens

things we think should be

with or without our participation

we know living requires work

a job to sustain our families

cars need gas, refrigerators food

we all need clothes to cover our bodies

in the heat and cold

cleaning tools and supplies

water has to be added

to remove dust and dirt

from our bodies, hair and clothing

who would believe

after this much work

in boycotts, marches,

underground railroads

riots, hangings, beatings,

stolen inventions, raids

killings, cover ups,

amendments, acts, addendums

marches, arrest, framings

unjust prison sentences

who would believe

our mouths would be full

of the same stories

more than seven generations later

in the beginning

fathers didn't hold their sons close

they were forcibly taken

to keep them separate

so many years later

fathers don't hold their sons close

is this history playing a game of tag

asking to be remembered

if we travel back there

to the time faulty records were kept

when on the list of property

or a ships manifest, captains log

only read boy, girl, woman, man

approximate age, maybe the area

they were taken or confiscated from

we can never find our roots

if we depend on that set of records

unless we swab our cheeks

offer a blood donation to determine

the origin of our bones

I find it repetitively sad

every other people or culture in America

know where they came from

know why they arrived here

they may have worked off a debt

but were not brought or bought

as a source of free labor

to build a country newly discovered

let's say you have a college degree

majored in accounting or mathematics

I would ask you to compute with interest

two dollars per day times thirteen million

times three and a half centuries

only compound the interest annually

I am not saying we are owed

every penny from the very beginning

but someone owes us every dime

from the very beginning

every other nationality

residing in this country

received payment with interest

for being treated unjustly

even the indigenous people

who were given blankets

to keep warm during winter

wouldn't survive the smallpox

hidden in the fabric until summer

later received some type

of compensation

I hadn't planned dragging

the old to this new

imagine your job owes you

back pay for months

and they are still calling

demanding you to work overtime

how would you handle that?

I am up for suggestions?

if the beginning

was spoken into existence

why can't we write

a new one for our seeds

hashtags and t shirts

don't seem to be able

to stop bullets, beatings

or societies mistreatments

we got words but no action

at least in the beginning

they had hard work with no pay

we got good pay but no work

not saying your job isn't work

neglected community support

equals no work at all

history has a way of finding

us where we sleep

tagging remembrance

every time we choose to forget

we are very forgetful

a lot of us act like we belong here

like we came here

of our own choosing

there can be no future

without knowledge of our history

of where we came from

and we don't know

where we came from

we may all need a shovel

to locate a shallowed direct connection

there are new flourishing communities

built on black cemeteries

head stones removed

shallow graves underneath oaks

there are places you wouldn't think

you could find yourself

I would guarantee the ancestors

never thought they would

find themselves in this lighted darkness

wearing a new language

here we sit centuries later

still trying to find the beginning

needing to dig up old tongues

to rediscover the origin

of our bones

there is no real future

without discovering our beginning

no journey completed

without a starting point

I think it goes back

to the beginning

before word split darkness

to form night and day

we were there

and are still here

trying to find our way to the light

It is time
we embrace
our differences
share our stories
write our future
love ourselves
and care
for one another

-ajh-

History From A Child's Perspective

as a young boy

I remember listening

to grown folks conversations

we were told to never listen

to the conversations of grownups

unless invited and to this one

I wasn't offered an invitation

they were talking about my cousin

her husband was a Black Panther

my only knowledge of Black Panthers

came with cages, zoo's and jungles

all of the adults involved

must have listened in

believed the medias lies

America often sold - repeated constantly

when members of the darker race woke up

became aware of the constitution

knew there was something wrong

America labeled them bad people

called them trouble makers

he had been arrested again

the common thing with him was

trouble, arrested and again

I never thought of questioning

trouble for who until now

he and some of his associates

were picketing Safeway

can't recall why they were picketing

the adult me knows

they were fighting for rights

the child I was didn't know

was suppose to be ours already

aware now, sometimes doing the right thing

will get you arrested

standing up for others will label you

a bad person, a trouble maker

I have discovered writing feelings

of the wrongs of this society

targeted to the black community

will mean I am writing slave poems

I don't provide answers when asked

why do you write black

how come all of your words

are fighting for existence

why do you feel as though

you are always fighting for existence

when I moved to Fort Worth, Texas

I was stopped by the police at least

twice a month, sometimes more

my children would ask

what did I do to warrant such behavior

I didn't know what to tell them

I would say hush

and let daddy handle it

not knowing if this would be the time

I looked like somebody

or a car like mine

was seen leaving a crime scene

I can't tell you how it feels

when explanations are not forthright

I remember as a child listening in

on the conversations of grown folk

telling myself I will never be

a bad person

no one would ever call me

a trouble maker

when you finally discover

what your legs are for

finally understand what rights

you are suppose to have

you will be just that

a bad person

labeled a trouble maker

there is a reason the world is round

a reason we keep coming back

to this Black verses America

this fight continues with no end in sight

I wish I could have

remembered sooner

created a war room

to prepare my seeds

being black is a fight

you will not be aware is coming

speaking out loud on the matter

most will consider you are talking

about slavery, mentioning occurrences

over four hundred years old

will label you a trouble maker

you will be called a bad person

do not worry

there is a long list

of bad people

who wore your last name

in order to fight for those

who are not aware

there is a war going on

you may have to become

the trouble maker

your ancestors were

the fight isn't over

bring everything you have

this battle will take a lot longer

than we originally thought

Nightmares'

to the mornings I wake in fear

afraid to hope those were nightmares

witnessed in the dark

I swear... they had the aroma of memories

the fire was hot, the tree was tall

have you ever felt the last gasp in your sleep

breath as cold as death

I didn't want to share

can't tell you how it feels

when ancestors remove your hands

and write for you

leaving explanations void of sound

every morning I have to check my bones

to see if they are still whole

have you ever listened as a neck snapped

under the weight of a man dangling from heaven

don't know if walking on air is possible

but no one has been successful

not in my family - searching my family tree

you will discover so many lives ended by trees

I am afraid to hope these were nightmares

scared of the probability

my ancestors want me to tell you

firsthand accounts before their eyes

were forced closed

there are stories in these cells

I would love to label nightmares

have you ever smelled flesh burning

my god... I hate to tell you

I know when you inhale

how it stings your lungs

how it peels freely from the bones

the hair is seared to scalps

as faces melt completely dissolve

fingers no longer look like fingers

I would rather these be nightmares

no one could imagine the souls of the fallen

bringing you enough pain

to block your prayers, kidnap your blessings

steal your hands and write their own story

demanding you read it

here I am trying to share it as dreams

but these aren't dreams or nightmares

these are the memories

my cells recall tales of horror

they could never write down

don't know why I was chosen

I didn't ask for this

no one in their right or wrong mind

would have strength enough

to carry these words

they couldn't travel pass lips

would trap themselves in your voice box

throats would collapse

even they refuse to tell this story

I must ask if you think you can hold on

to anything this slippery

so heavy it was discarded by time

only to be witnessed in the dark

there is a reason our ancestors

visit us while we sleep

no man or woman could handle

such conversations in the hours of wake

they've built padded rooms for us

all who listens - those of us whose hands

are removed while in slumber

tonight I will leave them a note

keep the hands - finish telling your stories

give them back when you are done

it is hard enough to carry the weight

of history, of all the things we know

I wish I could tell you with some assurance

these are dreams or lingering nightmares

but there are memories in my bones

messages in my cells transferred from souls

I break into pieces every night

feel parts of me moving through unfamiliar time

accumulating these notes, these truths of pain

it's up to me to read aloud

you will wish me committed

and I will second the motion

nobody said it would be this hard

but you can't find you

until you know where you come from

I got all these stories showing up

on pages in the morning I don't remember writing

my hands feel new, like I bought them today

I am afraid to hope these were nightmares

scared of the probability

my ancestors want me to tell you

firsthand accounts of life in apartheid USA

before their eyes were forced closed

there are mornings I am surrounded by shadows

an incomprehensible occurrence unless allowed by time

overlapped emotions will not rest well on pages

I did not ask for this - didn't want to share

there are few options if I wanted my hands back

need to read what my ancestors wrote

still praying for nightmares - wishing for dreams

but someone has to tell the story

just hope your time doesn't come

this is too much truth for one soul to carry

got me scared to sleep

Conversations With The Ancestors

before falling asleep

some nights

I request

the next conversation

with my ancestors

be with a child

a young man

preferably

one that survived

the darkness

I know I have them

conversations

with the ancestors

after the moon wakes up

eyes closed tight

these words

are not of my choosing

didn't originate

in the corridors of my mind

they must be a gift

I will accept blame

or any attachment

to where they land

they didn't come from me

and are not mine to keep

I can't imagine being taken

the few things familiar

vanquished in the blink of an eye

I just want to talk with him

he would be able to tell

of the journey

offer eyewitness accounts

of the struggle

I would rather hear

the whole story

remember his voice

using his words

trap them in my fingers

the words you read here

are not of my choosing

didn't originate

in the corridors of my mind

they are gifts to be shared

retelling the details

of any story

leaves out

the most important parts

the pain is merely imagined

the darkness

can never be written

dark enough

every sound is worth notating

if not all of them screamed

the silence had to be deafening

I've read twelve million

was an underestimation

can't fathom that many voices

crying at the same time

the earth would shake lose

its fault lines

oceans would rumble

not wanting to participate

water couldn't hold

this large of a burden

I really don't know

how to write this

how to let you know

this truth weighs too much

is too heavy to keep quiet

the ocean must be a cemetery

a single grave of mass proportions

an open burial ground

no one ever speaks

of the capacity of lungs

how floating to the bottom

how long anyone

can remain conscious

before reaching the deepest deep

how that dark

no matter how dark it is or was

can never be darker than the darkness

I bet you want me to hush

place gloves over these hands

force these fingers to stop talking

but who will tell the truth

when history keeps changing

in the books we are given

in the schools our children attend

they keep locking the doors

closing buildings leaving nowhere

for education to be found

I am left with no choice in the matter

I need to talk to him

a young man who survived

ask him how many times

his mind quit working

if he could hear every heartbeat

drumming, echoing in that darkness

how often his chest swelled

with memories

with the sadness of losing home

was he able to stop listening

to all that pain

with his hands bound to his side

if he remembered

how the food tasted

did he lose count of how many

didn't make the whole passage

could he still feel the warrior

in him breathing in that darkness

when they herded him to shore

when he stood on that wooden perch

when they sold him as property

as he was forced to pick cotton or cane

I want to use his words not mine

I may find out

I really don't want to know

but someone has to write this

has to tell this story

I keep hearing echoes

of people telling me

those days are past

it doesn't matter anymore

how they reaped the benefit

of hundreds of years

of free slave labor

but keep telling me

it don't matter

to this right now

I need to know

how I am supposed to take this

all quiet and laying down

like my ancestors don't visit me

ask me questions they ain't waiting

for the answers to

I don't need you to understand

not demanding you to read or listen

I got this story - I got to tell

or they won't leave me alone

I don't want to be left alone

but I'm going to tell it

like they told me to tell it

write how it showed itself

when it got here

these words

are not of my choosing

didn't originate

in the corridors of my mind

they must be a gift

I've been blessed

with these presents

so I will share

what I've been given

what you do with it

is completely up to you

Harriett

I bet on every plantation

there was literally a rainbow

of niggaz - every color

from the darkest purple blues

to the lightest tan almost white as sand

I bet you wonder why I wonder

bet you wonder why

I am looking round this room like this

there is this something inside I know

I can feel in my spirit at least three

yeah, three of you in this room

would have turned back

tried to ghost yourself

would've played sickly

talking about you can't

walk no mo further

thanking you gon sneak

on home to massah

like he ain't gone ask you

which way we left

what stars we following

like you ain't gon use them hands

and point massah our way

like you not understanding

if I don't shoot you dead right here

massah gon string you up anyway

gon make a message out of you

not a martyr - you gon be all messy here

blood everywhere or you gon be all messy there

bones everywhere, neck snapped all clean

tossed in the fire - they gon be no pick nic

it is pick a nigga and yous the nigga picked

like this culture of niggaz

these new niggaz, these old niggaz

starting out thanking they want some free

knowing they ain't got enough heart

ain't got enough beast in them

to go the whole way

there is a long way from right here

to that free you thought was right there

it will keep moving - keep bouncing

from person to person no matter

who you vote in - vote for - vote out

free is still a good piece from here

I wonder how many of them good niggaz

how many dem happy with dem scraps

how many of them called massah friend

Harriett had to pull the trigger on

had to lay to rest with everybody watching

necessity ain't never gon be easy

if free was gon be easy we'd a had

a whole mess of it by now

we'd be bathing in it

pasting it on the front of our t-shirts

tying it on the end of our locs

I don't know how many... but I bet

Harriett had to shoot

a bunch of you good slaves

wanting to ghost yourself

sneak on back to the big house

glad to tell massah

which way we headed

what stars we following

I think I'd been a gun carrier too

I would ask Harriett at the start

when we standing in rooms

just like this one

Harriett ?

I know you knows in the beginning

which of these niggaz

which of these good niggaz

which of these new niggaz

ain't gon make it

which of them gon want to

tuck tail and run

gon wanna jump and hide

in them bushes

like we ain't prepared

for everything

you ain't got to point em out

just look in they direction

I bet from here

we can still see the smile

of massah in they eyes

we'd see the glare

of fresh picked cotton

in dem teeth

we can take them shirts off

and hope we don't see

no yellow streak down they spine

just point em out Harriett

just look in they direction

I need as much practice

as I can get

cause we gon get some free

you and me

gon get there

whether these niggaz

these new niggaz

these old niggaz

wit us or not

we's gon get some free

Excerpt from the unwritten book
'The Book of Niggaz'

Charter 3 (Home)
verses 1: – 8:

1: most places had a name, we called where we lived our village, even visitors called it our village. We were all family, if not of the same blood we shared the bond of being human.

2: our medicine man traveled, healing the sick in all villages, our chief a great warrior; he was champion to many victories. In our village we never planned to call it anything else, but our village, thought it would stand erect for our children's, children's children.

3: the land was sacred, stories were told of its discovery. It was the greatest story ever told, everything we needed to sustain us was here. Fruit, soil bountiful, trees strong and tall, hunting was good. Our village was home if ever we thought of calling it home.

4: when they came for us, we were not prepared... no one knew they were coming. The wind paused as a warning, trees went hush but we were not ready. Warrior chief and medicine man always stood ready for battle. They fought as an army of two to give us time to gather the women and children to get them to safety. The fight lasted longer than the ones who came thought were possible.

5: when they fell, they would not let us honor them with the rites of passage. Their souls are still there waiting for us to come back. No one came back. What manner of man doesn't understand there is honor in battle, the fallen should be celebrated and welcomed back to the dirt from which they came.

6: our village was three days journey from water, we walked for seven, rest did not visit us tied wrist to wrist and right leg to right leg. Many fought to free themselves but there was no free, getting free was not possible.

7: we did not know who came for us and where they planned to take us. We passed villages abandoned, huts burned to ashes… we considered every one of those men, women and children our family too. No one knew what happened or if these were the same people who took them without us knowing.

8: you can live a long life and not know home. We will not know home again, can't see the trees from here, the souls of those not returned to earth will not know home. Our village will remain our village but we will not be there to grow the crops, to hear the dancing of drums, to teach our sons to be warriors, so they can learn songs of drums for the rites of passage. There may be no more rites of passage to teach them. We don't know where we are going or why… we know it will never be home.

Disconnect

I have been saddled

with trying to understand

how we keep hearing

but missing the message

the media places in plain view

we forget and remember

only when we are told

the blood of our ancestors

keep forcing my pen

to tell their story

too many pictures of new pain

revisits our days as old pains linger

begging for acknowledgement

I got a mouth filled with I'm sorry's

for those tired of listening

apologies galore

for all who don't want to hear

why can't we comprehend

until we connect the dots

we will believe none of these

occurrences are linked

are planned repetitive motions

we will be certain it started yesterday

pixels aren't pictures

until we see from a distance

remove your pride

this is not about you - it's about us

you can't be independent

when we have yet

to fight for independence

we must embrace our differences

to become the same

to fight as one

to even begin to change

our current situation

I hate being the bearer of bad news

but CHANGE ain't coming

she's been here for a minute

insanity is thinking

she is the illusion

you keep watching in thirty minute

and one hour intervals

as entertainment

the only thing being entertained

is your mind and time

idol or idle

I don't think or can't tell

and you'll never know

until you disconnect

there is no difference

This Is What Happens
When You Bootleg Freedom

if I tried to include

a list of the names

of all those

who died in the struggle

who were murdered

whipped with hands tied high

before being tossed

in the flames to burn

all those men and women

killed in this fight for free

it would begin - with the person

who saw the first ship approaching

coming over the horizon

right off the coast of home

this was before

before we became food for sharks

before we never had a chance

to say our goodbye's

to those too weak

to travel for months

living in three cubits in darkness

under the decks of boats

we are still too afraid

to pronounce the names of

before the forced

separation of families

before the changing of our names

before we were grouped by color

light or dark

long before cotton

or cane or whips and chains

before any means necessary

before we had that dream

I gotta tell this story

but I know you won't listen

cause pain always sings off key

the music of slavery

is too hard to dance to

the songs the slave sung

were too hard to dance to

ran out of that shuck

and all of that jive... years ago

if you watch me walk

you would know

we arrived here

with rhythm in our bones

there is a stack

of mildewed picket signs

resting in the back yard

underneath the shade tree

awaiting the next call to arms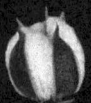

we got good feet

we's march good massah

we's march good

but words alone

cannot fight our battle

it is time

we not only learn how to listen

but what to listen to

you see this

this is what happens

when you bootleg freedom

when you are delinquent

on the mortgage

of your yesterdays

take short cuts to your tomorrows

borrow someone else's dreams

when you want a discount

on your babies future

we already know

our learning institutions

are teaching more how to pass a test

than how to read and write

they lied to you

been lying to you

for more than a century

told you… you could pay

for this revolution on layaway

you could lease a little taste

of freedom with food stamps

that rebellion ain't got no consequence

that them that's dead

was already proven guilty

told me my voice don't count

I'm still three fifths of a human

they look at me like I'm Attucks

like my family tree

only has nooses for branches

like I got a little Malcom

in my stage presence

like I'm just two seconds away

from the bullet on the balcony

like I run a crack factory

at that corner house

in my neighborhood

they look at me

like I filed the serial numbers

off all them guns

the police stations across America

say they buying but keep passing out

they look at me like I'm stupid

like I don't know the difference

between equal and unequal

sent them that look just like me

to get me

thought I couldn't tell the difference

between Black and Black

between Brown and Light Brown

between Niggaz and friends

between locs and weaves

they look at me

like they don't owe me reparations

like I lost my 40 acres

in a game of craps

like I'm not a fly

caught in the same trap

my daddy, granddaddy

and great granddaddy

got snared with

like I ain't putting in my best All

to raise my boys

like I got a mouth full of

Garvey's cry for freedom

in my raised black fist

you see this

this is what happens

when you bootleg freedom

when you skip classes

teaching you how to

rightly hold your purpose

when all you got invested

in the revolution

is a couple of food stamps

when Black

is the new color of targets

on these American streets

when you've been called

so many names

you lost your ethnicity

when there are no more

coastal shores

you call home

when daddies forget

what they sons look like

when you climb on stages

and your ears

are so used to bullshhh

like these words

ain't come to me

as a blessing

trying to save your life

Some Better

most days we treat it as though

it is the sixth or seventh

Monday of the week

there is always a distinct difference

in the way the sun shines

the clouds dance in the wind

a new dance

and out of our mouths

we wait to find some appreciation

for a brand new song

no one will ever hear the same music

we were made different for a reason

it takes each one of us

to make this day better

only if we are aware

it is our job to do so

ain't no blueprint for good

can't nobody make you better but you

I see you struggling to smile

like that breath you in and outing

is not a gift given you to smile for

we got blessings

we don't believe in sometimes

those fingers could stop moving

any minute now

and you ain't using them to create

your voice could leave you

it might quit anyway

if you don't stop

all that complaining and comparing

ain't no comparisons here

you got what you got

to get better at it

before it's gone

this is not a warning

it's a blessing in a message

while you still got sense

you might not even have that tomorrow

if you don't grab hold

and use some of it today

most days we think we can skip

over these lessons

side step these trials

like they not there

to help you find some better

ain't no such thing

as bad in your day

but there will be medicine

too hard to swallow

sometimes pain will attack you

just to wake your ass up

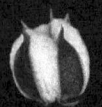

we've been sleep walking

a couple of years too long

nobody told us this was a race

in all seven lanes of this sprint

ain't nothing but you's

and how is it

you don't think

you can win

pride will have you

sitting idle at the starting line

not showing up for the whistle

hitting the snooze button

one time too many

this ain't no warning

life has never

offered anyone

an official warning

or presented a blinking

red light for danger

this is a blessing

in a message

while you still got sense

that could abandon you

tomorrow

if you don't grab hold

and use some of it today

Excerpt from the unwritten book
'The Book of Niggaz'

Charter 12 (*The Journey*) verses 7: – 12:

7: and darkness covered everything even our memories.

8: we lay locked in position, moving was impossible in the belly of the beast, hull hollowed enough to hear the splashing of bodies being tossed overboard.

9: I never prayed so much, so hard, for so long... every day was a prayer, we prayed out loud, in secret, in unison, in our dreams... we talked as though prayer, was our new language.

10: you could hear the sickening, listened as time choose them one by one. The longest after the first cough, the first sign, anyone lasted was three days, at least I believe it was three days. I learned to hear the rising of the sun.

11: every one of these days were long, longer than the human eye could see stretching across oceans, most of them seemed to have no end or beginning... just a middle lingering past dusk and dawn, we were captives.

12: surviving had little to do with lasting, the air was thick with stench, there was wailing and screams that begin to sound romantic, almost like music. Some cried until they lost their ability to speak. I prayed and hoped not to be the one to tell the story, no one wanted to be the one to tell this story.

When My Ancestors Come

some mornings

you won't feel as though the day

deserves your attention

no... revelry

you will not be welcomed

maybe fighting for daylight

is the perfect beginning

you will have to start somewhere

earn your keep

seeing another birthday is not a given

you've had enough free breaths to date

this nigga here

ain't got no mo jovial in his voice

f**ck jovial - can't laugh at your funny

most often you're only laughing

to keep from crying anyway

I am beginning to believe like Harriet

she said she would have freed

thousands more slaves

if they only knew they were slaves

I see you thinking walking free

means you got some free

there's never been nor will there ever be

a line passing out some free

or free for the taking

you've got to sacrifice something

the noose of knowledge

must be too tight

choking out your common sense

I hear chains rattling in your throat

see the cage and auction block

you keep balancing your faith on

if you think you will somehow

stumble upon the truth

you better fall quick

ain't no truth here

unless you brought it with you

and it can't stay

got somewhere else to be

all the rights and freedoms

others died for

are disappearing

by the constitution full

this ain't poetry

this shhh is life

and you think

every time I speak of our history

everything is a slave poem

you and America

are constantly fooling yourselves

keep telling the same lie

until it is easy to swallow

until it taste like truth

you can't see the picture

while enjoying the pixels

colored so gracefully in crayon

stepping back to get a better view

never crossed your mind

I wish you had picked some cotton

wish you knew how long it took

for open lashes on your bare back to heal

witnessed a hanging or stood helpless

watching an angry mob drag your

son, daughter, wife, husband

or whoever you used to love away

knowing ain't no coming back

when these rights are gone

they ain't coming back

we didn't arrive here by choice

and we still struggle to survive

that hush in your mouth ain't surviving

you've been frightened quiet

too scared to open your mouth

there is always silence before a hanging

before a murder, before the coroner arrives

I can hear your heart beat from here

hoping you and no one else is listening

afraid them satellite's will spot you in the crowd

you can't fight sitting down

can't punch with your hands in your pockets

with no pen in your hand, with no paper to write on

you patiently thinking this is not your war

but whose is it - if you don't fight for you

there is a long list of excuses

we remember from text books years ago

don't quite know when we got em but we got em

and we use them waaay too often

you may think this day can make it without you

it can but you won't survive till dusk

you probably thinking

this is just another slave poem

like I'm not trying to help you, help me, help us

you got to do more than march against murder

signs won't stop the killings

posting comradery won't change your jail sentence

won't even get the murderer's

extended vacations cancelled

if this is just a slave poem

I will keep reading it

until the ashes come to life

until my ancestors come home

I bet they got some shhh to say about this

they will see you consciously unconscious

spitting bullshhh trying to sell

some t-shirts - I can't breathe

forgetting this system

has been choking our ass

for as long as we been here

we've always mattered to us

ain't no slogan for fighting

ain't no song gone make us dance better

this ain't no ballroom

it's a slaughter house

they killing in these streets

and you sitting in the comfort of your house

I wish my ancestors would come

set fire to the alarm clock in your bones

so you could wake the f**ck up

and stop being so consciously unconscious

if this is just another slave poem

I think you ought to listen

think we ought to be screaming it in unison

we should all know the words by now

before we all be wearing chains again

singing old negro spirituals

with a chorus of 'We Shall Overcome'

in poetry venues

sanging bout'

how we gone get us some free

Action

looking at horror movies

I mean frightening stories

the scariest and scariest of tales

I mean the national and local news

it all appears as horror movies

there is a fear factor

for young and old black men

walking at night

or in the morning

driving to work

or on his way to lunch

sitting behind the wheel

at a red light, stop sign

making a left turn

or signaling to make a right

driving the speed limit

in a residential neighborhood

enjoying the invention of

cruise control

two miles under the posted limits

in the slow lane on the expressway

parked peacefully at the lake

on a college campus

minding your own business

catching the bus

riding the train, taxi drivers

often will not see you

waving your hands

will not notice you screaming

in their direction

won't see you whistling

can't see you running after them

with so much yelling in your voice

the whole world is afraid

of any black man

with so much yelling in his voice

every black boy or man

is the potential next scene

in a horror movie

no script necessary

we were born with others

able to read the lines - written deep

in the complexion of our skin

we teach our sons

America's theaters and producers

are searching for the next black model

the leading actor who will not make it

past the opening scene

name will not appear in the ending credits

Wes Craven should be here

sitting in the director's chair

he never uses crime scene photos

or caution tape

in his movies, the villain

will always be brought back to life

you should hear a faint cry of

five, four, three, two... Action!

as you close the door behind you

take a good look, say a nice good bye

this could be the last time

your scene may be called on

you could perform your last dance

you won't pick the song or the place

America always has first dibs

on black boys, old and young

for more than three hundred years

we have all looked like boys

in sit ins - in organized rebellions

a million of us marching

standing in Washington Square

living in the White House

listen close or you won't hear it coming

five, four, three, two... Action!

in our scenes

in the movies we star in

directors will never say

CUT!!!

How Can You Listen

I keep forgetting to ask

who are we marching for today

what t-shirt am I supposed to wear

what name should be on the front

where can I purchase a readymade sign

these are the things we don't know

until somebody tells us

until it's posted on Facebook

tell me again why we are not voting

why don't we care who the judges are

in our communities and districts

why do we let so many positions

for representatives and congress

go unopposed - are you listening

tell me why we will video fights

and not stop the violence of these youth

why are you mad at the person

once considered your closest friend

why don't you speak anymore

why is this venue so much better than that one

how can you listen - how can we hear anything

over the defaming of victims in the media

making it their fault they changed lanes

were attacked while jay walking

looked like somebody else

got caught walking in the dark

with his head covered

there is so little truth to discover in lies

so many lies completely void of truth

I can't hear you over the sirens

over the last Amber alert

sound can't climb, can't jump high enough

to rise over the crime scene

I can't make out your words

while bodies still lay uncovered

in the middle of the street

yes, I am angry - but I'm not yelling

I have to speak louder

how can you listen

I know you can't hear me

with my hands raised

over the echoing gunfire

from Ferguson to Texas

from Baltimore, to Oakland

we can't and should never get used to

shrieks of ropes tightening in prison cells

or a mother's tears at a news conference

explaining her son wasn't violent

he was going to college

he didn't have a knife, it was just a toy gun

Lucie's are not Drug Cartel's

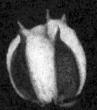

they don't deserve choke holds

I thought breathing was a part

of this American dream

how can you listen, when its America

telling you what you hear

my ears keep getting misdirected

from the last sermon in your mega church

you didn't grow in the community

the building fund was meant to grow

I thought college campuses were safe

were ideal for learning

cars don't attend classes

missing license plates

are a matter for the courts

should not be a death sentence

I am sorry to keep asking

what are we marching for

what new chant, new song, new mantra

are we whispering today

they can't hear us on the next street

one town or burrow over

in the next city or a state away

I want to get this right

there is too much blood in the sand

on this corner, in this parking lot

on the sidewalks of this street

to stay on this path

which way are we going

which way are we headed

where are we

leading our children to

I am afraid to change lanes

don't want my life to get crossed

we are thirteen percent

of this nation

quickly on our way to eleven

I used to be so good

at mathematics

until I started counting bodies

how can we listen

when it is impossible to hear

over the screams of our daughters

assaulted at pool parties

how can you listen

when we are all speaking at once

when everybody already has the answer

I am angry

but I am not yelling

I apologize for asking again

who are we marching for today

what t-shirt am I supposed to wear

what name should be on the front

Excerpt from the unwritten book
'The Book of Niggaz'

Charter 18 (of Water and Rain) *verses* 27: – 33:

27: the day they gathered us to leave our village; it rained, not the rain you pray for hoping the crops will grow... it rained. If the medicine man were here, he could explain to us the wonders of sky and rain. This was no rain I had witnessed before, it fell hard as if it never planned to cease. I could hear murmurs, all sounding the same, the sky was afraid they would take it too.

28: I believe on that day the sky cried. It bellowed and yelled, we didn't know thunder could be so loud. We all believed it was the God of water announcing disapproval, even He did not want us to leave our village. There was no shelter for us, drenched, wet with tears and rain, no one was familiar with the direction we were heading. All we knew was fear, and from the sound of the sky, it was unhappy and very much afraid also.

29: our village specialized in all types of fish, big fish, sharks, every sea creature we knew how to prepare. We were all swimmers since birth.

30: three days of every week we would gather together before the young warriors would go visit the ocean to gather fish. We prayed to the God of oceans to keep them safe and bring them back to us with enough of everything the ocean had to offer. They always returned, so we knew the God of oceans listened to our prayers.

31: on this day we see in front of us ships of different origins, we prayed to the God of oceans to hold these ships here; send help, we knew if others knew of our demise they would hurriedly be on their way. We only asked for the waves to push against shore, to beat against hull and give us one more day on this familiar earth to find a way out.

32: hearing the wind rumble we thought our prayers were being answered, but no help cometh; alone we must discover how to untangle these ropes, these ties that bind us. In my mind I know we are survivors but not just survivors we are conquerors. The waves never came, they didn't rise or force themselves forward or retreat, the God of oceans must have been too busy to listen.

33: some never made it aboard ship, would rather visit the God of oceans themselves, took all tied wrist to wrist with them to the bottom; we never saw them surface. I thought of my seeds watching me a warrior tied to other warriors; humbled to the point of tears, without any possibility of escape, what would become of them? I must survive for them, conquer the fear of the unknown, no one knows what is waiting for us on the other side... we have known since we learned of stars, there is another side.

Where Is The God In You

sshhh!

there are children listening

how will we teach

these young men to be men

if all you wear is boyish ways

change your shirt

where's your tie

pants shouldn't be

as low as dresses

or as high as skirts

underwear goes under

they are supposed to be covered

we walk like Europeans

with an Egyptians head dress

locs meant knowledge in your head

will inexplicably be entrenched

in your walk

we were God like

not beings of this earth

where's the god in you

have you forgotten

men were hung

beaten, disrespected

sold as chattel

so you can hold your head up

have you forgotten

women were sold

on auction blocks

treated as chattel

raped and made to watch

as her children were taken

forced to mother those not of her bosom

so you could hold

your head up

how could you forget

when Ferguson, Fort Worth

Fruitvale, Fort Lauderdale,

Fort Hood, Boston

and Baltimore looms large

our communities spiral out of control

our freedoms are under

arrested development

we've lost our rites of passage

sentenced to silence

in our own court of opinion

we slaughter more of us

than they will ever unlawfully kill

there is no more middle ground

too many of our sons

rest below ground

others withstood

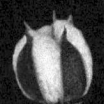

so we could withstand

they were held down

while we hold hands up

before the attack

was with water hoses

and dogs - now its tasers

bullets and blue gang beatings

how dare you share

your blasphemy

negating the respect

of my father and ancestors

with your degrading of our women

with lyrics, videos and poles

raining fist filled with dollars

calling them hoes

as though they still

stand on auction blocks

dancing for cash

while twirling on poles

like in massah's kitchen

or behind locked bedroom doors

in cotton field bunkers

on store room floors

as though they are still chattel

where's the god in you

you say you pray

but your knees look new

where is the God in you

you say

we're in this fight together

why only against blue

how can you forget

the struggles

and the pains

we have made it through

where is the God in you

at least pray for us

even if you don't

care about you

find the God in you

we slaughter more us

than will ever be

murdered

by those in blue

I am willing to fight for us

but first what you must do

is search yourself

for I know it's true

I can see from here

there is still

a lot of God in you

Sentry's of Sand

I think it was last year

after arriving in Dallas

for my mother's birthday celebration

family always gives the best hello's

our greetings last as if

it will be the last time

sometimes you may hear

a faint goodbye in the best hello

a prayer of safety

in the how have you been

two of my favorite nephews

treat a jail cell as a saloon door

it swings back and forth

they travel back and forth

in and out of this prison system

as if it is an apartment complex

and six by nine is adequate space to live in

only one of them were present

the other was visiting his second home

if anyone can call a prison cell home

I gave him the tightest hug

these arms could give

without forcing the love

I have for him into cracked ribs

this was the moment I realized

for the first time

an uncle's hug could never equal

a fathers embrace

there will never be a substitute

I am not sure why I believed a present me

could substitute for an absent he

I wasn't aware there was a war

raging furiously on the same street I used to live

we shook hands as we spoke of yesterday's

and future plans - his palms felt coarse

I could feel the rails of all the caskets

he had the hands of a pallbearer

his grip was strong

I could only imagine from practice

of holding the weight of empty vessels

he gripped my hand tightly

as if trying not to drop his friend

he was too accustomed to walking

in more funeral processions than hallways

I didn't know there was a war going on

on the same street I used to live

he was receiving his GED behind bars

I knew then he attended

more funerals than classes

grew accustomed to carrying

more caskets than books

there will come a time

you will discover

words are not enough

and love is not a shield

to defend him from himself

the more I looked around

the more it became apparent

on every corner it seemed the stop signs

were hung at half-masts or half-staff

these corners were grave yards

they are a weigh station for corpses

he could tell more stories

of lost life than happy days

I didn't know there was a war raging

on every street by my mother's house

I knew the sons of friends

who thought slanging and banging

was the quick way to rise up

only to discover

it's a quicker way to lay down

I tried to explain

you can't claim the hood

if you don't own any dirt

you can call it home

if you don't put in the work

how can you teach

your sons to be men

if you spend so much time away

failing to show your worth

in this neighborhood - in the dark of night

the youngest angels carry guns

the police sermons sound more pretentious

of the preachers who left

than the drug dealers that stayed

I wasn't aware there was a war

raging on the same street I used to live

first you notice a boarded up window

next the closing of businesses

abandoned houses, new liquor stores

too much caution tape on sidewalks

too many outlined bodies

in the middle of streets

some wars don't come with warnings

sometimes there will be more silence

than the bursting of bombs

even the sky felt disgraced

how could a country

how could churches

how could pastors

how could fathers

leave these seeds unplanted

hoping they could grow themselves

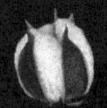

too much wasted blood

to raise a white flag

they would consider it

an act of aggression

would claim it a weapon

if we moved our arms

we couldn't surrender

no one would notice

the cameras were waiting

needing a story

wanting for the perfect lead

to highlight the 6 PM

the 9 PM, the 10 PM

breaking news reports

to capture another shot

of another shot

of another shot

its hunting season

dark and light skinned boys

are the prey, the trophy of choice

there is a war going on

in every community across this land

you can close your eyes not to see

but this could be our last stand

we can't stop the violence against us

if we can't stop our violence against us

Talking Drums

there were over

thirty five thousand

chartered round trips

to the mother land

on a quest to retrieve human cargo

a venture so profitable

hulls of ships were retrofitted

to maximize the number of bodies

each could carry, listed on the manifest

was the number of acceptable losses

in lieu of all this planning

I guess not one of them

were equipped with space enough

to transport drums

not one djembe, junjung, Ngoma

Bougarabou, Aburukuwa or Bata

made the voyage

we've all heard tell stories of messages

of information transmitted

from village to village

in conversations with drums

how certain rhythms spoke of war

a particular collections of beats

were used to worship our ancestors

celebrate the birth of a child

the arrival of a visitor

these were talking drums

it is believed in this age and time

every person born of African descent

first breaths are in beat

arrives with rhythm in their feet

a song in their throats

inherent melodies carrying legacies

we have always been a spirited people

there are things our ancestors

had to recreate in secret

upon arriving to this new land

it wasn't by invitation or for vacation

they were not attempting

to escape a regime

or the horrors of home

history denotes it was not by choice

it was strictly for profit

the early church didn't allow drums

didn't allow slaves to shout

it was too reminiscent of the villages

they were taken from

at the close of Sunday services

the slaves would form a circle

repeating a line of a song

taught them by their captors

and shout

the men and women

would celebrate

dance and shout for hours

inviting the ancestors to join

their voices became the new drums

you can strip a people of their names

of their families, clothes, traditions

destroy memories of their culture

but never darken the glow

the beaming light of their spirit

no matter how many chartered ships

or how many sovereign benefactors

benefited from the sale of dark skin

their voices became talking drums

they used a borrowed language

songs teaching subservience

chariots meant... trains or wagons

angels... were people carrying lamps

or safe houses, porch light burning bright

the slaves sung

on the ship on their way here

sung while chained in line to be sold

sang on their way to plantations

sung while picking cotton

sang after being whipped

the brutality given to any slave

for trying to escape

we still call them negro spirituals

but they were the drums

of the spirit in negroes

undying, unwavering unmatched

we have voices for drums

spirits centuries old in our hearts

we can sing new songs

taught us in the language

of our captors

place in them secret messages

generations old of overcoming

clasp our hands together

from a circle around the globe

dance, chant, shout

just as they did upon arrival

for days, years or however long

it took to send the message

bid our ancestors welcome

we have so much work to do

if we will ever gather

forgotten parts of our history

to form a path to enlightenment

it will take all of us

to find our way

Roar

she asked me if I knew

the story of Lions

if I knew my locs

resembled their mane

I used to think ancestors

placed lions teeth

underneath my mother's bed

before my birth

a ritual of chiefs foretold by griots

she asked me if I knew

how Lions teach their sons of life

what plants are poisonous

what fruits are best

how to capture, protect and feast

I tell my sons these streets are jungles

do not fear this place, you live here

know there are those wanting to capture you

to place your teeth under their bed

hoping their seeds will grow to be Lions

know how the chase works

even when you're not running

how threatening your Roar sounds

when you speak hello

I tell my sons of survival

there are traps in this jungle we live

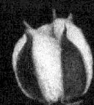

your mane to me is precious

you are a King

the prince of all I am

she asked me what I knew

of Honor, of Lions, of Roars

I told her this stage

I share my truths from, is home

sometimes my poems sound of Roars

I am no visitor to jungles

I was born here

teeth of great ones

neckless I adorn

worn by Kings before me

I tried to explain the silver

heaven painted in my mane

I will grow it until I earn gold

heaven knows I am worthy

I teach my sons of caring

just being a Lion is not enough

for your jungle to survive

you must care as kings

must walk with pride

she asked me if I knew of Lions

how Roars sounds godly

a language of its own

my sons and I talk

in Roars sometimes

we stride through this jungle

as proof we live here

and are not visiting

jungles are not safe

unless we make it so

I am learning more of Lions

of why my mother needed teeth

under my birth bed

why my father walked with me

through the jungle

as proof we live here

I teach my sons of my father

how history's lessons

remain intact for ages

we are centuries of Kings

of Lions, of Roars

our jungle shrinks

but we still live here

we must be proud of our mane

and how we walk with sons

I know of Lions

now I must learn

more of life and me

to teach my sons

this life of jungles

The Black Book of Black

Excerpt from the unwritten book
'The Book of Niggaz'

Charter 26 (No More Sun) *verses* 81: – 88:

81: if I would have known while being prodded, beaten and forced on this ship to no one knows where; that would be the last time I saw the sun. I would have paused, waited, took in a bigger glance to hold the rays close making them unforgettable.

82: when darkness surrounds you, when you live in a place absent of light... your eyes will learn to see through the mist of black. Living in a village, nothing will prepare you for the absence of sun. It took a long time, maybe weeks, to adjust my eyes to silhouettes, to fragments and figures moving about in the black underneath where we lay as close as twins, as inseparable as married couples.

83: laying still for days, it is believed some died and came back to life hoping the dream had ended. But this was no dream, no nightmare, a reality not yet realized, we were captured not by an enemy, unknown forces came and took us from everything we knew to be.

84: all of our bodily fluids excreted lay next to us, we can feel them, smell them, I learned to appreciate the darkness. Feeding was out of necessity we never knew what we were eating, some days it seemed to move about in the pan they tossed my way, I ate it anyway, hunger is a beast no man can tame.

85: there were women of my village, whose bellies were swollen with life, we planned to celebrate the joy of birth, but here we lay bond, surrounded by darkness. What right has anyone to bring the joy of a new born into existence, not existing themselves. We do not feel alive, after each birth there is moaning, gnashing of teeth and cries of pain. It is the mother duty to not let her child bear the burden of the darkness we find ourselves in.

86: she would yell each step of the process. I would cover my ears if my hands were free, shut my mouth if my mind would listen. The mother yells on, *"it's a boy, he feels heavy like a warrior should. He should not know this place, should not learn to see in the dark... his life cord, I am wrapping around his throat, I will not let him cry, he will not know pain, will not even know he was here... let us pray."*

87: to the God of oceans, of air, of trees, of all we know to be... take this warrior child from the darkness, bring him into the light, never let him know pain or the black of black death we have in here. Teach him the way of good, we have nothing here but bad, accept this love and our sacrifice, for we have but one option, to send him back to the God - he comes from.

88: then there was silence, not quiet but silence, thicker than the black of darkness. We were all ashamed, we could not protect him, could not welcome him in celebration. We know not where we are going and afraid we will never again know our village, or anyplace to call ours. We are captives, unlike any one we have ever conquered, these men know no God, have no honor... we prayed for our own doom.

Matters of Fact

everyone is aware of the percentage

the Black population holds in America

able to quote the imbalanced prison statistics

and has known for many years

justice bares the innate flavor of being for just us

there are also the common points to make

most of the drugs used to fight diseases

were not created for the disease it is battling

is not a means or method of eradicating said illness

most often the percentage of acceptable loses

has already been enumerated

patents and formulas are bought and sold

on the stock market and Nasdaq

it is all for profit

the drugs distributed in impoverished communities

did not come to form in any of the communities

said drugs are being sold

there were no labs or pharmaceutical facilities

for us to conduct such transactions

or business dealings

how and when they arrived

was more than likely

deleted from the records

in ninth century China

after the alchemist

made the first batch of gunpowder

called huo yao

which was used to treat skin infections

but worked better propelling lead

to inflict bodily harm

thousands of years later

in our communities, in our hood

we thought unity obsolete

so bodily harm it is

there are no factories to produce

gun powder or guns

 in our community either

how they were made so readily available

will be a discussion for a later date

and you wonder why we get so angry

when someone else guns us down in the streets

has to be we are jealous

we are accustomed to doing that ourselves

we have almost killed more of us

than America placed on the front line

of all the wars in which she's been involved

I wonder how it would sound

just on my street if the ass of jeans

were not dragging on sidewalks

if the bass beat in your car wasn't covered with

slanging, stacks, jacking and sex

boasting of conquest and raining dollars

as if the children down the street from me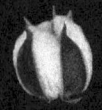

and the ones that used to live

down the street from you

eat breakfast before school

or dinner when they get home

imagine the harmony if conversations

from eleven year old's sounded more

like children and less like sailors

if fun was filled with more laughter than bullets

if a house party could just be a party

with no need to call the coroner

I have a problem with us

we can easily identify the problem

someone else brought to our community

but not accept the blame for the detriment

we inflict on ourselves

America taught us well

we've read of treaties with tribes

of indigenous beings - owners of this land

long before visitors placed the flag of ownership

on the front of their lawns claiming discovery

we marched for free

but weren't willing to fight

we accept the unacceptable

as though we refuse to put in the time

to force change

how long will we sit idle

eyes tight shut hoping

when we open them

there will be a rainbow

of change greeting

our fake smiles in the morning

we wait not knowing in essence

waiting has always been putting in work

comes with that blood, sweat and tears

we used to read about when we used to read

an act of servitude even in biblical days

I got a problem with us

got our throats on repeat

when anyone says

these words are repeatable

not all words are repeatable

when are we going to stand up for more

than paying ten percent in a place

that really doesn't need your ten percent

it's not a bad thing to go

but it has to be considered bad

if all you ever do is go and not do

I got a problem with us

talking more about doing than doing

making plans we have no plans to keep

dreaming the biggest dreams

only when we sleep

and you wonder why we are still

in the same place we've been

since the last assignation

since we celebrated whose ever birthday

we were told was a great leader

only after they made him a target

when they've shown time and time again

if you are willing to fight

bring the kitchen sink

they've been fighting

long before we knew

there was something worth fighting for

ain't no free unless we take it

ain't no unity unless we build it

shake off the hate and blame

we've grown familiar with the taste of

ain't no us until we wake up

be the voice to raise the Lazarus

we've been tomb sitting for too long

as a matter of fact:

we love to claim it ain't just us

but whatever happens

in our communities

have always been - just up to us

Dark and Darkness

I could never imagine

so many months of discomfort

rocking back and forth

riding unbalanced waves

chained to anything

hard as wood - flat

with no pillow to rest my head

I close my eyes

cover them with my hands

for as long as possible

wanting to embrace the darkness

but everything I have ever read

of the darkness our ancestors survived

that measure of blackness

had body and form

so thick you could taste it, feel it

heavy enough

to blanket your memories

forcing forgetting, giving up

and acceptance, easy to grasp

nothing in this day and time

would be an adequate comparison

most of the people I know

do not believe in ghost

through personal experience

The Black Book of Black

I began to question this belief

at about eleven years old

I will not speak of the circumstances

or pose the particulars for debate

I do know everyone asked

believe we all have a soul

no matter how we label it

the inquiry had no relevance

to any religious doctrine or faith

once while on vacation, touring caves

used as a hub, an island center

for the housing of slaves

until being transported and sold

my emotions got the best of me

a lump swelled in my throat

rendering me speechless

didn't notice my eyes were leaking

until my hands were drenched

my feet instantly became anchors

body felt shipwrecked

legs stiff and unforgiving as a board

I could feel the weight and pains

of history clawing at my soul

knew the burden of discovery

this remembering

will not be easy to carry

finally understanding this load

is not just for me

it is for us all

most of the people I know

do not believe in remembering

love the challenge

of stripping time

and memories of color

removing any reference to slavery

cleansing writings of all facts

they don't believe

history carries weight

there are structures

we pass in the south

seldom offering

a second glance or thought

never questioning

who owned the land

or who lived there

before being claimed

as county or state property

remarketed for purchase

these structures badly weathered

but are still standing

some used to be slave quarters

others, minority developed communities

their foundations

a labor of love

hand erected walls

roofs tattered

surroundings excavated

fragments of history

remain intact

each one reminds me

of chains and shackles

proportionately spaced

staked deeply in cave walls

of every size imaginable

smaller ones for infants

the thought of it

takes my breath away

what if souls of the begotten

will not leave

cannot move beyond

the space where suffering

became common place

the exact spot they took their last breath

what if those souls are charged with the duty

of battling winds, rains and weather

for preservation of these slave quarters

of shattered minority communities

to aid us in remembering

mandating we not forget

there is pain in remembering

eyes all of a sudden

may leak uncontrollably

history will always carry weight

along with the responsibility

of holding fast it's truths

we are not required

to believe in ghost

to know

these things happened

without conscious or records

without notating or documenting

so history would remind us

some pains cannot be written down

some words are too heavy

to sit on pages

we must remember untold stories

of massacres used to silence

those on who's backs we stand

this burden of discovery

will not be easy to carry

is not just for me

it remains here

for us all

Hell or What?

watching the news

and the constant feeds

in the mediums

in which we waste time daily

made me aware

I didn't know how bad it was

I didn't know how bad it is

I don't know when

the planet stopped dreaming

when the world stopped believing

I've seen men wearing crosses

faithless

talked with those exiting synagogue's

with so much hate in their speech

bible study in churches

are not safe anymore

I remember not so long ago

four little girls died in a church bombing

we can add nine more to the story

and believe me

tomorrow

it will just be a story

I don't know when

this planet stopped dreaming

when the world stopped believing

three fifths of loving someone

is built of believing in them

the other two fifths

is made of dreams

how together

we can conquer the world

I didn't know how bad it was

it is even worse now

than the witch trials

more verbal slaughters

than during the inquisition

I watched as she

snatched her love back

I could see the invisible

particles of love in her hand

through her words of disbelief

its getting bad out here

when the first amendment

is treated with the last rites

of a funeral service

don't ask me how I know

I just know

I heard people screaming hate

the other day

while holding a sign

filled with scriptures

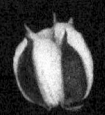

standing on a street

not far from my house

Texas is a big state

but this was right next door

here we are still debating

if dark equals light

if a child with melanin

should be treated

with the same respect

of other children

not blessed to have it

I don't know when

this planet stopped dreaming

when the world stopped believing

I didn't know how bad it is

she stood five feet from me

as doubt leaped from her tongue

as though it waited

until the proper moment to lunge

doubt is a bundle of bullets

targeting your faith

believing needs movement

needs a push forward

sometimes my hands are tied

some days I am tired

from pushing forward

you can't believe

if you're not moving

can't faith

with doubt being forced

into your ears

I didn't know

how bad it could get

what you think

of a situation tomorrow

will be determined

by the writer who wrote it

I want you to get how bad it is

you will not hold these moments

in memory and label them

the good old days

what if the truth is

there are no good old days

when assassinations

are days we celebrate

when every poem sounds

of machete sliced from the reader

when the best words you hear are

death, left, gone and tomorrow

when every week

we create a new slogan

place it as the bull's eye

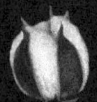

in the middle of our chest

praying words will stop the butchery

I don't know when

the planet stopped dreaming

every religion

places tomorrow's dream

in scriptures

always speaks of a better life

how heaven is better

how hell is so much worse

I didn't know how bad it is

some days

it's just missing heat

but this

this be hell to me

we need to start believing

and dreaming right now

if we expect the next sun

to rise on some better

whatever your better may be

you best start believing

pushing that belief forward

cause ain't no better coming

if you don't force it

and tell it

when to get here

Excerpt from the unwritten book
'The Book of Niggaz'

Charter 48 (Next) *verses* 22: – 28:

22: we are not living here, after we were herded from the ships, they separated us from our families, lined us up by height and weight. We were cattle, beast of ownership. No man should be the owner of another man... they gathered us in droves, as men of wealth does meat for sell. One by one we were forced to stand on wooden perches, naked, afraid of what could be next... not one of us knew, what could be next.

23: I watched as they poked my warrior son with unclean hands, felt his private parts, caressed his muscles, bent him over to see inside. No father should witness such horrors, no man could stand idle as his seed stood in humiliation. **Sold**, I heard him say... **sold**, how could anyone call another human property, place him in the open for others to choose. I didn't understand the tongue of which they spoke; but **sold**, I knew and **sold,** I could not understand.

24: I have never felt such pain, my refusal to move was greeted by the sting, by the ripping of flesh from my back, unlike anything I have ever dreamed of feeling. My warrior gave in at the next pop, the sound of flesh ripped away, it was cold and hot at the same time. I grimaced and stood where they placed me. Men and women grabbed my arms, touched my legs, caressed my private parts... I felt ashamed, the warrior in me, held his head low in defeat. I am losing this war and we just got here.

25: it was much worse for the women, they felt them up and down, opened their legs, inserted fingers and pinched their breast. I had to turn away. I couldn't watch. It was their bodies being violated, and I am sure... they couldn't watch either.

26: I tried to remember my village, all I could see was the darkness of black they dug me out of. How can I not see where I came from? We are not living here, our eyes just met the sun again for the first time, such an unwelcomed sight. There will be no life after darkness, although the sun shines bright - this place, this pain, this crowd remains absent of light.

27: amazed I stood watching, as they forced the warrior in my son out of him. I couldn't watch, but could not force my eyes to turn away. Thoughts of my village will not come to me, this may be the last time I see my son less the warrior I helped him to find. Another pop, and I was awakened from the place my thoughts took me, legs would not move from the wooden perch. I am now property.

28: man owned by man, I cannot understand. How a warrior can move from honor to humiliation in any span of time. There will be no life after darkness, only a life of darkness. We were not prepared when they came for us, and nothing could prepare us for the dark. Next is a place I am not willing go, this is not living, I am convinced there can be no life after... no sun, after all those days of darkness.

Questions and Answers

I wanted to write a poem

in the voice of my father

answering all the questions

the way he would have

had I known

I would need to know these answers

had I known

how to verbalize these questions

if back then I would have had a clue

I would require such words to place

directly into the memory banks of my seeds

a child at play will never notice how time

has no starting pistol or starting point

how time moves on

whether you pay attention now

or wish you had later

no linesman will ever say

take your mark

you won't be aware

this is a race for everything

no winner take all

or loser go home

this is life, the only race

the only one you have

it is impossible to go back to then now

or drag this now back to then

to show him these scars

lay flat the crumbs

of what used to be my heart

tell him love is that b**tch

you should have introduced me to

when we sat playing dominoes

in the back yard

or should have had your friends

tell me about her

while y'all were drinking pluck

and slamming bones

under that shade tree in the front

or pointed her out in the crowd

when you and all your friends

were Stagger Lee drunk under the bridge

you taught me to drive before I could run

but didn't teach me to love before my first kiss

I wish I could curse like my father

tell you to f**ck it and f**ck you in the process

let you know

I wouldn't give a cripple crab a crutch

if I had a lumber yard

and take the shhh from a blind

tumble bug and put him

on the wrong got damn road

how every morning I would prefer

to slap the shhh out myself

to get this day started

cause I don't like

and don't give a shhh about nobody

my father had all my friends laughing

at his memorizing antics trying to memorize

the words in his sentences, I have yet to hear

anyone else say them right

in the army the drill sergeants were always

angry at me because I corrected them

told them Jimmie Jay Houston the first

would not take kindly

to you f**cking up his life's work

these coy sayings he passed on

for entertainment

I wish back then

I had these right now problems

I would ask him the solution with chest out

he always told me

to speak like a mutherf**cking man

hold your head up - look me in my eyes

that's what real men are supposed to do

I want to answer the way he would

if I had known these were real questions

most children seldom ask their parents

how their childhood was

what their plans were growing up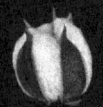

if attending college was a thought

how did you choose your occupation

if I was planned or accident

I could see his hard work

but didn't know

what drove him to do so

didn't know when he discovered

necessity is a carefree b**tch

that couldn't give a damn

what your plans were

where you planned to go or do

I would ask how he stood strong

the day he was extricated

from the church and choir

I remember him saying f**ck you and you

I will see you at my house soon

my wife still plays the piano here

I don't ever remember seeing

a lump in his throat

you know the one

appearing so often when your pride

is too large to swallow in a single gulp

when you attempt to force your tongue

to make anger disappear

when you know the listener

didn't see the punches

sound will deliver

my father had fist for lips

every word leaped out in the direction

and hit the target of anyone

they were aimed at

his friends expected nothing less

they knew he would correct them

would be the one to give truth

whether they needed it or not

just because they were friends

when a son discovers

his fathers sacrifices

were not because

his father loved sacrificing

there will come a time

need overshadows want

your actions will determine the outcome

I wish someone had told me to ask

wish I knew how to look closer

to see the cuts were not self-inflicted

they were scars formed over years

finger scratches from days of battle

struggle and death are both undefeated

the best you can do is hold your ground

you will not know

what you're in need of

until the need arrives

staring you face to face

when the fight comes

knocking at your door

backing up or down

will not be an option

you will not choose to

but you must act

had I known I needed

to know these answers

how to verbalize these questions

if back then I would have had a clue

I would require a powerful message

to place in the hands of my seeds

it is impossible to go back to then now

or drag this now back to then

I remember friends

sitting at the dinner table

didn't know that could have been

their only meal for the day

I see now building a community

has more to do with people

than buildings, young eyes

are not trained to see wisdom

no matter how smart

the child, some of these trials

are the returning wars

my linage, my family

battled long before I arrived

and will be here

after I am gone

I don't know what

I should have asked

but I am sure

there needed to be questions

if you still have a chance

to ask your father anything

whether he was there for you

or more ghost

in your fondest memories

ask him

you will need the answers

polite ain't necessary

this is the only life you have

you will not know

what you're in need of

until the need arrives

standing right in front of you

face to face, with mountains for teeth

knocking at your door

Heaven and Home

I think most of the songs

referencing heaven meant home

and some of the home verses

were talking about heaven

in Cuba the life expectancy for each slave

only rose to single digits

history states the presidents

and business owners during that time

invested heavily in continuing

safe passage for ships

transporting human cargo to that region

while in America the life span

for slaves was much longer

but heaven no matter the reference

always sounded a lot better than here

anywhere sounded better than here

contrary to popular belief

just because they were singing

great day songs didn't mean any of them

were having a great day

even back then motivation waited

on the edge of tongues to arrive

keep giving yourself the message

you wish to receive and soon

you may be ready to listen

taking into account receivership

does not in turn make it so

it leaves so much work for the receiver

we still sing songs of heaven

got me wondering if I listened

if I heard any of the words

some days I don't want heaven

to be my home

and pray my home

ain't nothing like heaven

there were many code words

hidden in verses back then

we will never be able to interpret

writers had to use tales

and second hand stories

to convey as much as we know already

which should mean, we don't know much

the captors wrote as if

they were mostly on their best behavior

any discipline was warranted

needed to be instant

it was his fault they hung him

he failed to understand he was property

and wasn't authorized to leave

she was pregnant because

she was property and not able

to control or be in charge

of her own body

such a simple explanation

when put in the words of your captors

history has purposely omitted

too much truth not to call it a lie

and it happens to be one of the main

requirements to receive the paper

given to say you have spent at least

twelve years of your life

being properly mis educated

even today we sound like them

Malcolm said "Massah is we's sick?"

noting how the slave owner feels

so does the slave, and we still sound slavish

like we will run back ever so often

to check on massah to ask him, is we's sick

we often forget we are owed reparations

but act as if we owe America some more free

we got too much old times in us

to act like we are new

to turn that other cheek one more time

as they were taught, as we were taught

as we teach our children

I haven't learned how yet

how to explain, what a cross burning meant

I know what it stood for

but if they were Christians... God fearing

men and women and Jesus died on the cross

why was the cross always on fire

shouldn't they have taught us that particular passage

it seemed to always be in full effect

to convey their message of better

I always force my pen to not add religion

to stay clear of frightening other Black folk

but if scriptures were used to keep us slaves

why are we so comfortable wearing chains

shouldn't there be some scriptures to free us

 one we can put on repeat

at the rate we listen, it may take

a couple of generations to catch a good ear

I am not saying we still wear chains

but it is hard to tell since they are created

by the latest designers - we wear wireless ropes

around our necks, trees are not used to hang us anymore

our pants rest around our ankles, don't fit our waist

slaves never had new or designer clothes

on every plantation their pants didn't fit

we follow fashion - this need to be included

has us trapped in a new type of bondage

I want to write some new heaven songs

with some new songs about home

I want the songs of heaven

to be about heaven, and the songs of home

to really be about home

this stolen language has us always

speaking in code, sending mixed messages

we use words in the same context

the way we hear words being used

we don't know what we are saying

we don't even sing great day songs

most mornings the music is about

guns, hoes, head and money

dollars black owned businesses will never see

our communities will never share

I want us to go back to singing

some heaven songs

and some songs about home

I want us to know the difference

between being free and owning freedom

I want us to write a song about

what we should call ourselves

because we can never be a unified people

never become a nation united

if we don't know our own name

and can't tell the difference

between heaven and home

The Slave Trees

in grade school my friend Freddy

told me his uncle was moving to Texas

he worked in the orange groves of California

he could take all the oranges he could carry

sell them on the corner

he was underpaid labor

made enough wages for a meal

but not enough to feed his family

his uncle called the orange groves

slave trees

I've heard and read of trees

cut down, carved round

perfectly trimmed, equal in height

replanted deep in this earth

wrapped tightly in barbed wire for branches

this is where Nazi Germany

grew internment camps

but most would say

it was surrounded

by an army of slave trees

I remember stories told

of buildings unkempt

of Hell's kitchen

of dilapidated tenements

of unbalanced books

The Black Book of Black

for indentured slaves

the building absent of foliage

were still called the slave trees

I have watched America teach our youth

through the planned design

of glorified superheroes and villains

with a history of numbers and digits

tattooed across their forearms and wrist

in remembrance, in holy homage

of camps, circled by carved round trunks

wrapped tightly in barbed wire for branches

I still see them as slave trees

but I've been told

not to speak of one way trips

or shackles, of middle passages, or ropes

say nothing of the rapes or beatings

told me there was never

a separate but separate

told me King and Abraham

were fighting the same cause

that black on black

is merely ethnic cleansing

but I know why weeping willows

petitioned heaven

to change the dimension of their branches

they could no longer bear the burden or blame

America places on trees for lynching's

it is the trees fault

their branches are thick enough

high enough, strong enough

for bodies to dance on ten inches of air

weeping willows asked

if their branches could be leaves

thin enough to sway, to dance with the air

if they could leak water, make tears fall

for the many souls of those wind dancers

prayed they could never be cut down

could never be turned into wood

to make crosses

they knew no one would ever

call a cross what it is made of

no matter how high the flames

no one would see a slave tree burning

told me not to speak loudly, of Crows or Jim

of this system misteaching our young

from pages of what used to be bark

never say a book could be a slave tree

just keep blaming the Oak, Birch, Magnolia's

Maple, and Gum for their aide

in helping black bodies

defy the laws of gravity

keep blaming the tree

for it is our fault, three fifths

makes almost a whole, but wasn't enough

no was always a yes

we couldn't own any dirt

I've been told, to never speak of slavery

not to make mention, of languages lost

this is a new day

pay no attention to the wind

Weeping Willows are lazy

they are crying for nothing

their branches sway because they can

they are not dancing, a dance of relevance

do not wonder

how many other types of trees

stunted their own growth

afraid to be burdened

scared America would blame them too

for lynching's, say it's the trees fault

for being just thick enough

just strong enough, to help black bodies

defy the laws of gravity

lies will be written on their flesh

historical records won't reflect the truth

even the trees, are worried for histories sake

for nothing in this world, wants to be remembered

or reminded, it was once called a slave tree

Excerpt from the unwritten book
'The Book of Niggaz'

Charter 62 (Afterlife) *verses* 136: – 150:

136: everyone from our village, after being drugged from the wooden perch, knew they would never know peace, or life, or family as we once shared. There is a reason they placed us in the darkness, memories seldom survive even when light returns. There was no way to tell the time of day, it was forever night. You could often hear the unshackling of chains, the dragging of bodies of those whose sickness overtook them. In some way or another, we were all sick.

137: as they pulled me from the wooden perch, I counted too many to remember, would have offered them greetings and safe passage, but chains are stronger than rope, every woman, man and child were taken in different directions, as if separating our language became the goal of our captors.

138: there were eighteen of us, all speaking a different tongue, belief and faith anchored in a different God, our thoughts were not here, we did not know where here was... the look of bewilderment on our faces could never tell the whole story. Would there be life after the darkness? or just black thoughts, in the heat of this sun. We were bound together with chains... wrist to wrist, ankle to ankle, rope twisted tightly around our waist... we could feel the pull and tug of the wagon, each of us prayed to whatever God we believed in, asking Him to invite us to the great hall when life has left, begging Him to take us from this place... we all knew there can be no God here; if so, how could He sit silent and watch such horrors.

139: we moved constantly with no rest and very little water, some fell and were left where they lay. The men took the responsibility of making sure the women and children never felt the lashes of our overseers, they took pleasure in the sound of flesh ripping from our bare backs. How can any man take pleasure in such atrocities when we were not at war, and didn't know the source of their anger.

140: many treacherous miles and three sunrises later, we could see in the distance a structure unlike any I had ever seen, although my bones were tired and eyes were weary, I could see clearly, images with the same hue of skin I wore, moving about. There were men watching over them. This must be where they are taking us, I can't understand anything the people in the wagon or on the horses leading us are saying, and can't make out any of the words those I am chained together with are saying either.

141: how will we communicate here, all of us speaking a different tongue? How can we become family, after watching all of the family and culture I knew abandon me in the darkness? There will be no understanding here, no peace, only struggle and pain. Listening to the yells and watching the movements and gestures of the men who seem to be in command, even their language sounds broken the same as all of us, it must be stolen. I doubt they have anything they didn't forcibly take from someone else.

142: young children are running about this place in their age of innocence, the warrior in them asleep, I cannot awaken the warrior in me, we have just arrived here and he feels defeat is inevitable. How will we communicate, this is not living. We are forced to merely survive, if anyone can brand this surviving. There are no oceans here, it has not rained since our arrival… the God of oceans must be furious we did not perish, our God must believe we did not do everything in our power to remain on our sacred land and let them take us. This is the reason none of my prayers have been answered.

143: the earth is not willing to give in; the ground is hard, looking at the position of the moon at night it is planting season. They are not skilled at growing and do not know what they are doing, their way will not reap to fruition the crops we are made to sow. I will not mistreat mother earth because I am being mistreated, she deserves to be reverenced, no matter the place I find myself. I will till and make fertile this soil, so at least one of the God's will know I have not lost my way.

144: upon our arrival, we were herded to an area surrounded by men, they removed the ropes from our waist, disconnected the shackles from each other, but returned the shackles to my wrist and ankles. The wooden structures we are forced to live in are not living conditions, but it is more comfortable than the darkness, better than not knowing next, if this is next, surviving will be important. This unfamiliar terrain will make it almost impossible to find my son. I watched his warrior leave him, I know he knows how to survive in the jungle but there is no jungle here, and seeing another day's sun may not mean you've survived, it is just a new day of darkness with uncertain light.

145: we once stood on sacred ground, understood our place on this earth, with oceans and in the skies. Trained our seeds to be warriors. After a life or months of darkness, we do not know where we stand, this feels like another earth, it will never be our village, we are not sure if the God we believe in, came here with us.

146: every man, woman and child here has their own horror story, we are all in shock. No one knows which direction their family was taken or if they are still alive. Most cry and scream through the night, so loud it reminds me of each new born sent back to God when we lived in the darkness. Some may wish to still perish. I speak often to the warrior in me, asking him to return. He has not answered since our arrival. I was born warrior, half man, whole lion but there are no jungles here. How does one survive in an environment not meant for survival?

147: if the griots from my village could see me now, telling the story of this trouble... they would say I haven't lived enough moons to be a great story teller, I would have to agree. Being the oldest to survive the darkness, who would bear the burden of this pain and be able to tell the story? There is no one left to share the history of my ancestors, my grandfathers will be forgotten, where I come from will not be remembered. I must tell of this place so all will know, there is no God here, just pain, work and heat, we may not survive but must do our best to live.

148: every morning I say my name out loud, in honor of my father who named me. Batchagui Arioch, Batchagui Arioch, Batchagui Arioch, I am not sure if I will remember it tomorrow, my back may not withstand the remembrance. Every day they ask me who I am with lashes, and tell me who I am with lashes, one day soon, I may only be who they tell me to be.

149: we eat for nourishment never knowing what it is we are eating. We have no choice, if tomorrow will greet us with as much work as today, we must eat something. The sadness can be overwhelming, smothering those not strong enough to withstand the memories of missing loved ones. I have watched sadness break men, take away the breath of mothers whose seeds vanished from her presence. The only thing in existence after the darkness is darkness, pain and sadness.

150: I am not sure if I should write much more, if this story is worth telling or if anyone will believe such atrocities occurred. I stopped praying to a God who will not listen. I believe everyone here stopped praying also, knowing no God could hear us over the cries in our hearts. No man should wear the burden of telling this story for histories sake. We are all warriors here, but not one of us can summon their warrior to save us. Our warriors are still standing on the wooden perch, struggling to survive after the darkness or be sold into bondage under this new sun. We will surely perish in this place, or wake up one day soon being only who they say we are.

Dirt

fashioned from clay, made of earth

a quandary for scientist or religion

I do believe we are made of

the same place we go in the end

Dirt

I mailed letters to random places

different people in the many countries

in the region of Africa

enclosed a small container

with a self-addressed stamped envelope

I only asked one question

could you please send some of the earth

directly outside of your domicile

I don't know where I come from

but I am trying to find home

I ended each letter with sincerely yours

and thank you very much for your help

as the packages arrived

I placed distinct markings

describing each country

and the person who gracefully

followed through with my request

then removed a patch of the existing grass

I wanted the new earth to feel as if it belonged

I wanted this house to feel like home

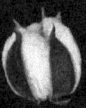

I don't know where my bones came from

sometimes they feel lost

they long to stand

where my ancestors stood

I know the procedures and process

for erecting new houses

the earth is transported from sites

from landfills to fill the land

I don't know where, this dirt came from

my feet feels it is unfamiliar

every time they are greeted here

I don't know where my bones came from

don't know what region of Africa

my ancestors were taken

I just want this house to feel like home

I always walk with eyes closed and bare feet

across the new earth, need to become familiar

the textures are different, so many images

dancing in my mind of faraway circles

of unity, of a time I can only dream of

I want this house to feel like home

I want my seeds to know there is a difference

in how your toes respond to earth

your bones consider family

there are a few places my feet will pause

for what feels of minutes, but could be longer

as if my bones remember

this marrow is trying to remind me

my blood pumps slowly

comforted in the moment

I must believe this

is what home feels like

when you know where you come from

but these bones are clueless

they've been wondering

for years

wishing for an eternity

even my eyes view earth so differently

always asking the question

forever needing to know

how it would feel - really feel

to plant these feet in earth

walk on dirt

the same as my ancestors

if it would feel like

heaven or family

if I could walk and feel

as if I am dancing around a fire

if I could stand still and know

this dirt

these grains of sand

this house is home

This Is The Last Time I Fix Broken (2)

death - dying - killing - murder

we have grown accustomed

to how death looks

shared in high definition

in brief intervals

by news cameras, cell phones

excerpts from video clippings

none of the stories are whole

we digest only the palatable parts

like vegans - like tall tales - like fables

sliced up edited versions

of the best lies they can sell

truth as absent as a two year old's front teeth

I remember the first names of so many

flashes of brilliant, black, young - unarmed

talented teens, young men

wearing so much promise

the same old, new American story

retold and retold until it loses its newness

remembering first names is easy

they all had last names too

and parents, who planned to watch them grow

didn't plan to plant their seeds for God to grow

didn't know blue, was the new color for Jim Crow

too many years early

too many missing sons

too many cemetery visits

too many lives done

too many code blues

too many drawn guns

I have to fix this broken, before I lose my sons

there was another killing yesterday

he wasn't even safe at home

don't know how they can twist this story

when another black life's gone

we can't just talk about it

can't keep it up in here

like this is a church or synagogue

where we can hide our fears

they say God help those who help themselves

I don't know about you

but I am writing a plan to action

to do what I gotta do

I will rally all the ones

who don't think they need to vote

and those who visit the church house

ask them for food and coats

and Monday go to the homeless shelter

to give to those who are broke

we can't start fixing this broken

like it just got broke today

there are decades of broken shhh

we covered - thought it was packed away

we got relationships need mending

we got fathers who need their sons

we got communities missing guidance

we got businesses on the run

we got religion that need some fixin

got preachers needing to walk their word

we got communities where the U is missing

we got pain that ain't being heard

we were taught how to break shhh

and how to take working things apart

we never learned to make shhh

or how to love with all our heart

this is the last time I fix broken

it's impossible to do it by myself

if you can't see the problem

there's no way you can be much help

what if broken can't be fixed

and you think all this is for naught

we can no longer entertain negatives

if you've yet to give it all you've got

there is so much death around us

not to arm ourselves, put on armor too

I am ready to fix this broken

I can't wait too long on you

Cotton

every year, same day

it comes

the lost theory of forgotten

usually it starts right past midnight

on the 19th of June

I can feel the Sam Houston in me

too afraid to shake my family tree

I have no idea what or rather who

would fall from its branches

I've heard, one of the last slave traders

in this country, wore this last name

my father learned me to be proud of

all I know, is every year, same day

my thoughts rustle for clarity

my mind plants this weary in my bones

I guess it feels of cotton, if these hands

could remember what my grandmothers said

they always told me, lost stories of cotton

how it was poetry to pick and not get pricked

how on good days

Damn!

if you can imagine, cotton and good days

dancing in the same sentence

I got a whole lot of battle in me

between this name Houston

cotton - and good days

I know the story of the Alamo

how it was twisted to fit in Texas history books

I know even this, wasn't a war or glorious battle

this fight wasn't for a building poorly designed

and half-finished... this was also for some free

of them slaves they recaptured and traded

for some acreage and that good Texas sand

them slave traders were getting

all of what we know as Houston, for black bodies

as long as they could walk and stand

free labor is free labor, especially

when it comes to that pure white cotton

I know how long Texas can hold on to truth

before they send a General or Congressman

to tell you the parts they want you to hear

I would rather believe the average tongue

would roll out and spill words as heavy as Free

you can go - sorry we forgot

go find your family

this telegram of freedom

got tangled in the wires

this message from Washington

got scalped on its way here

it's hard to believe something

pure white as a little ball of cotton

could hold this much truth

this much battle

I've heard one of the last slave traders

in this country, wore this last name

my father learned me to be proud of

this lost theory of forgotten

got me remembering

got me shivering lose

this Jimmie Jay in me

these be my father's thoughts

I tremble in these bones

every 19th of June

cause truth

ain't got no easy travels

on days like this

don't even know

where to land when it gets here

some ears can't listen

can't drum this truth

since we forgot our drums

left them on the shore

I am Texas proud

but I am black man mad

ain't no balance in this body

when you know

and don't know how

to tell those that don't

some of them

don't want to know

too happy with not knowing

there is this

lost theory of forgotten

we could build a fire

and circle dance

on the 18th of June

right afore

that day gets here

like we used to

my bones tell me

we danced

long before we came here

walking on this Texas dirt

I got this lost theory of forgotten

usually it starts

right past midnight

on the 19th of June

I can feel the Sam Houston in me

too afraid to shake my family tree

I have no idea what

or rather who

would fall

from its branches

Just Wanted A Passing Grade

in biology lab at Kansas State

the assignment was to write a paper

on the study of genetics

the pristine neatly typed pages I turned in

were immediately declared unacceptable

my instructor placed on top a failing grade

smiled as she told me apologetically

failing this class would mean

I'd be repeating biology

back then I didn't have this me

able to care what people thought

I met with the dean of students

explained for the whole semester

everything I said in class was scrutinized

everything I wrote usually turned into

an open debate to be disproved

handed him a copy of my treatment

"The Long Term of Effect of Slavery

Both Mental and Physical A Study of Genetics"

it examined how America

delves into the history of mass murderers

suicide victims, violent criminals

most all of them void of melanin

analyzes their family records

for latent traits in their DNA

using their findings as a reasonable

determination for said behavior

I didn't have any proof

but I know sometimes my dreams

are not dreams at all but memories

that somehow attached themselves

to the double helix resting dormant

traveling from person to person

for years or maybe centuries

before wrestling with the conscience

of someone deemed worthy of listening

I am not claiming to be worthy

but I have learned the art of listening

new findings in any form of science

are not easily accepted

unless the institution you received

your doctorate or masters from

authorizes you and your research acceptable

I on the other hand a mere scribe

who believes in the power of words

with undying faith in his fingers

acknowledging most of the things

forged in sentences by these hands

were not conceived in this body

sometimes my soul orders me to write

I oblige - wishing to call it conjecture

say it was me who thought

such scribblings a good idea

assert somewhere in my mind

sleeps a great thinker

but these are troubled times

I believe our ancestors

will do whatever is necessary

to inform us, to let us know

this isn't our first walk down this street

it is not the first time

black boys began to disappear

are being slaughtered where they stand

not the first time our children's bodies

were found with no internal organs

we are always the right blood type

hearts, kidneys, lungs, livers

appear on hospitals waiting list

next to the name of the richest of donors

I couldn't understand her anger back then

the look in her eyes as she read my treatment

wanting a good grade is a battle sometimes

not knowing the full impact of the message

wish I could say I knew it would be controversial

would be an honor to boast it was done on purpose

it was just an assignment in biology

I needed a passing grade on

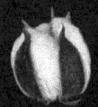

you won't be aware

of what you don't know

you know

may not see the ocean

in a drop of rain

notice the blaze

while enjoying the heat

can't see the blood

in the glistening of diamonds

no one ever notices

a snowflake in an avalanche

you will not hear the whispers

over your next heartbeat

as clear as day

we all have them

moments of clarity

no one really knows

where they come from

how they appear upon arrival

it is just a look and see thing

thought more people

would understand

everyone looks the same

as my biology instructor

there is no old and new

just done before

these things have been done

so many times

the missing children

the unexplained deaths

claims of aggression

a targeted back

demanding he was

coming toward you

I only wanted

a passing grade in biology

didn't think the memories

could scare awake

anyone who took time to read

there is no old and new

just done before

we need to start building

new soon

this done before is killing us

the dean of students

spoke on my behalf

wanted to know

if he could keep the copy

graciously I nodded yes

and happy

I didn't have to

retake biology

Complicated

the Emancipation Proclamation

didn't end slavery or free the slaves

it was intended to disrupt

the economy of the south

a flourishing industry with little overhead

no cost for labor only small fees

for the replacement of slaves

rebellious, fighting to get some free

it's complicated

explaining how a document

written with such urgency

did not include slaves owned

by the author, it granted freedom

to slaves residing in defiant southern states

willing join the cause of the union

it's complicated

if we searched every continent

to find a group of people

the same race despising themselves

or rather each other

unwilling to work together

to benefit themselves

or rather each other

we would only find such people

living in America

it's complicated

how we prefer to invest

in businesses owned by any other race

than invest in ourselves

or someone wearing the same skin

for generations we have been told

doing business with family or friends

will never be beneficial

not to trust anyone

who looks like you

just those who don't

it's complicated

deciphering the path we took

to become so self-centered

hating ourselves, disoriented

fake hair, fake ass, fake eyes

fake smiles, fake family

fake car, fake house

we own very little

but spend everything we have

to mirror ownership

a passion for borrowing

with no plan of returning

no one knows how we arrived

at this place of disunity

why we will go broke

changing our inherent features

mutilating our identifying qualities

is complicated

pick one

African American

Afro American, Black, Colored,

Negro, Nigger, Slave

we have worn as many monikers

as we wear suits and dresses

keep changing names

as if not one of them

were worthy of wearing for long

it's complicated

not knowing where we come from

impossible to tell the truth of our arrival

no stories of our grandfathers grandfather

except the ones no one wants to hear

we are the only people told to forget

forget how we got here

forget how many suicided themselves

to avoid making the journey

there is too much pain to remember

too much struggle to forget

we don't know what to call ourselves

lost would be perfect

it's complicated

having no culture to lean on

we will test fit them all

no religion so we swap tales of glory

taught us by others

with hate in their speech

picking Gods over Gods

faith interchangeable

it's complicated

finding out faith can be

so easily interchanged

taught an early lesson

thou shalt not form

any graven images

so every image engraved

doesn't look like us

it's complicated

learning how to believe

but not in ourselves

how to share but not with ourselves

how to love but not love ourselves

learning all this history of others

not of our ancestors

and none of ourselves

it's complicated

not knowing how to uncomplicate

our complexed addition in this society

unwilling to include the whole of us

we are perfect at three fifths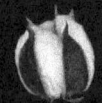

two fifths stills stands on the shore

awaiting the next boat

it's complicated

no matter how much truth

we hide in the words we write

it will be viewed as a lie

explaining how a caged mind

in a freed body renders you still slave

we are still in need of free

not from chains but psychologically

it's complicated

knowing the pursuit of higher education

can lead to more miseducation

we have centuries of experience

in missing education

we have families still in wait

to declare the first in their history

to graduate high school or attend college

we follow traditions unaware of their origins

celebrate nationally birthdays

of the leaders they assassinated

we gave up our businesses

at the invitation into theirs

it's complicated

not understanding

we can't build an empire

without building our community first

can't teach other children to be better

without teaching our seeds first

it's complicated

after more than one hundred years

we remain rivals

field niggers darkness

against house niggers brown

for getting we all be but niggers

in the eyes of those in charge

pick one

African American

Afro American, Black, Colored,

Negro, Nigger, Slave

the only way to un complicate

our complexed addition into

a society we are waiting

the proper invitation to join

pick one

what's in a name?

our ability to construct an empire

when we finally choose

but it's complicated

History In 76 Lines
(from beginning to new beginning)

in the beginning

if we could ever determine

when and where the beginning began

history has a way of deflecting

the origins of everything written

if directly associated or mentioned

with the continent of Africa

very few references appear

in the system we rely on

for education, for knowledge, for truth

the greatest psychological findings

advancements in science and astrology

were attached to Greece and Egypt

the latter after it was torn away

from the corner of Africa

we have learned to claim discovery

of land, technology and people

if their skin and culture differs

America labels them savages

or third world as though

we do not all live on the same planet

his story will simply reflect

occurrences viewed in the eyes of captors

what and how they believed it should be witnessed

the writings of history

will never get it right

doesn't matter how many drafts

of the constitution you read

how many times

you repeat the preamble

how you interpret

the Monroe Doctrine

or Louisiana Purchase

how many Bills of Rights

were evoked

or how many prominent northerners

invested in Cuban plantations

or how many presidents insured

safe passage for charters

from Africa to Cuba

or how many Acts or Amendments

attached to the constitution with intent

of making us feel included

inclusion is not an attachment

added as an afterthought

ever so often a discussion must ensue

a process of ratification

giving us the right to continue to vote

it may feel as if Plessy verses Ferguson

stands true in this present day

there is so much history

we don't want to know

and couldn't find

if we searched

if we could ever determine

when and where

the beginning began

how do we keep forgetting

we are the same

different country

same continent

various shades

of the same skin

we are the same

from struggle to pain

from ancestor to present

from ship to shore

we are the same

red blooded visitor

to this place we call home

this is the same fight

same battle - same struggle

our ancestors struggled with

it is mandatory we rediscover

togetherness, unity

and a new beginning

Takeaways

African American - termed in 1899, intent to give a base for discovering our history, all human beings of African origin.

Afro American - first records show it was the name of a newspaper published in Baltimore in 1892.

Black - became the name of our people and a source for Black Pride in 1968, given validity in the number one song on the charts for six weeks, by James Brown and Alfred "Pee Wee" Ellis. 'Say It Loud - I'm Black and I'm Proud'.

Negro - a description and term decided by the dominant white majority in the late 1800's.

Colored - it was used before 1900, but became popular after coined by the NAACP which was founded in 1909.

Nigger - too many conflicting sources on the origin of the word, but it's use is considered derogatory, no matter who uses it or the context for which it is used.

Slave - an estimated twenty million were taken from the continent of Africa, the numbers vary. The United States presented the most abusive form of slavery in the annuals of history.

Charter - over thirty five thousand sponsored round trips made the voyage to Africa to retrieve human cargo. It is the reason the title of each excerpt is charter and not chapter.

Cotton - one the main agriculture items used to build economic value of both America's and still traded heavily by many continents, now using machines to pick and separate its parts.

Ancestors - a genealogical reference for tracing or relating family history from the origin of a bloodline.

The Black Church - dates from 1758, the first slave owned institution able to own land. It is viewed as the savior for Black people in America, this association considered by members of white society was the ultimate threat to their existence.

New Drums or Negro Spirituals

Pens are the new drums, a syncopated beat echoing the human condition when words are placed in songs or any poetic form of expression. No matter how clear you place the message no one will ever get the same meaning from your words. Spoken word, poetry, slam are the new negro spirituals... let us sing a resounding song echoing across the Atlantic, the Delta, the Mississippi, Texas, Georgia and all surrounding borders. Become the message and the messenger... Let us sing of Uniting, this is our new song.

Peace Be With You

Ase

Amen

Shalom

Later

We Out

The End

Did you know something as small as a ball of cotton could hold this much TRUTH?

About the Author

Writing poetry began early, his mother encouraged him to write. Whatever he passed to her whether written on a brown paper bag she said was good. Maybe that's where it starts, when you begin to believe you are actually good at something. Not that you are good at it but someone else believing and encouraging you in the endeavor has to be inspiring. His hosting and performing skills dates back to the second grade in Dallas, Texas strangely his first starring role he was a doctor of punctuation, fixing words and sentences, his next feature was the rabbit in 'Alice In Wonderland'. There is something magical in the noise of silence when the audience is listening. He has performed poetry and hosted events since the 1980's. He has written scripts, directed, worked behind the camera and co-founded one of the first Minority Owned Productions companies in the Dallas Fort Worth Metroplex. The shows aired locally were "Impact With Willis Johnson", "Sound And Style Showcase" on channel 33, channel 21 and channel 8. The last two shows were a Poetry based show shot in a club formerly known as Blue Cat Blues located Deep Ellum, Dallas the house bands were Common Folk and Yarbrough and Peoples, and a comedy based show hosted by a famous comedian at Vocurea (spelling incorrect) located in formerly Red Bird Mall that never quite got off the ground. No matter the journey writing has always remained at the forefront. For AJ Houston Poetry has always been life, life has always been Poetry.

Acknowledgements:

The most excellent thing about this book is I had a crew of listeners and readers. I am learning to listen myself, attempting to get better at receiving constructive critique and use the words given to become better at this poeting thing we do. I am honored and wish to personally offer my sincere gratitude to Faye Marie, Jahmal Clark, Janean Livingston - Freeman, Mother Craddock Chuck Jackson, Anthony Douglas (Mahari), Priceless Black, Ester Van Hutchins, Akil, Minnie, Angela, Alex and Dominique would pause every now and again I thank them truly. When your sons take note it is truly worthy of notating.

To my mother Birdie Lee Houston and my other mother Mrs. Geneva Conner, both of these great women were very instrumental in my love for words, the reason I believe in the thought process and grateful at their arrival, to my brother and sisters, all my seeds, friends and associates. I am all in on gathering the lessons life has to offer, write them in poetry form and hide my pain and joys in the middle. I am grateful to every venue for letting me share the stage with other great poets. The list of friends and loved ones would cover a couple pages so to all of you I love and thank you for your support and prayers.

To everyone who purchased any of my etchings, framed poems, chap books, came to events hosted and preformed. Thank you... Thank you... Thank you. Send your comments, responses and any errors you find to: *poetajhouston@gmail.com*

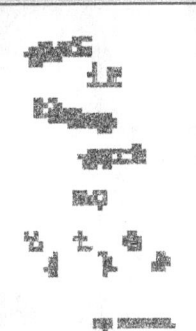

New Titles Coming Soon

Not Yet Lost *Jan 2016*

F.A.C.E. *June 2016*

(Fibromyalgia Awareness Changes Everything)

The Legend of Shrenk *July 2016*

Lost Pens

(A Pocket Guide For Writers)

all books can be purchased @ amazon.com, or at the next performance to receive a personalized signature. Booking and contact information can be located on the last page of this book.

Contact Information:

njalphabets.org

www.twitter.com/ajwordartist

www.facebook.com/ajhouston

www.youtube.com/ajhouston

www.reverbnation.com/ajhouston

poetajhouston@gmail.com

Additional Products:

CD 's   Love Seasons - The Awakening - Whispers

Coming Soon Books

The Legend of Shrenk

Not Yet Lost

The Fireplace

Talking With Angels

F.A.C.E.
(Fibromyalgia Awareness Changes Everything)

T-Shirts

Poetic Lessons

NJA Gear

Poet's Supporting Hunger

For Booking: Contact

AJ Houston

@ *poetajhouston@gmail.com*

www.ingramcontent.com/pod-product-compliance
Lightning Source LLC
Chambersburg PA
CBHW051943160426
43198CB00013B/2280